Sad Face

THE TRAPS

Sad Face

CONTENTS

One

Two

The secret of poetry is cruelty.
                    —Jon Anderson

(wild snap-dragon)
in a hot lane;
                    —H.D.

ONE

THE TRAPS

Missy gets tied to the rafters.
She likes the lack of choices,

I'm afraid: one, solitary
hummingbird
per zip code.

She dreams
she breast-feeds blood
she dreams of faith.

What did you know about fire?
& where did the blind one put it?

BLUE COGS OF A SECRET

I thought of you in those woods,
what they did to you there.

How a memory—(fur, being charred)
must be stubborn, or quit.

At the deep end of the pool, two
Down syndrome kids

took their bathing suits off.
This won't happen again.

& her body is blindingly right.
Stick a pickax through it.

POSSESSION IS 9/10TH'S OF THE LAW

Once this notion was felt; enclosed
me in a jar. So what

if wings were bloodied, at the cage.

Over Salt-Creek again, over Wolf-Lake.
The hyphenated world does pirouettes.

Alone with that. And only what I know.
Somewhere on this sweet Earth

it is summer.

ADMONISHMENT

To be impossible, but full

of endless mouth. Same goes
for hissing starlight in the daytime.
You hold

the slippery kitten 'til it says
let me eat

somebody else's music now.

THE 10:15 TO CAMBRIDGE

Maybe twin violets have reasons.

They say there's a world
that keeps on coming up with springs—can you count

the times you've seen it
on one hand?

But I wish you the swirling grace of London swans.

That the oncoming train
was a pack of the shyest white horses.

ALTERED

It's like the hankering for land, before she touched it.
Balsam axis, where the length

of this occurs. A little stubborn weather
in her system (the perforated flowers,

half-moon surge). Now, she stands in doorways,
willing gulls

to rise. Such a sorrow to their efforts. Gale
wings tithing. No

arrive.

FUTURE TREES

Bracelet-ed in the ozone,
they are not here to entertain,
disseminate
leaves.

As if a man is speaking underwater.
You're owned,
and thus, you're charmed.
Quid pro quo. Ever think
for every bird

we've bred this terrifying syntax?

SNUFF

You can exit the city of ghosts. You can't exit
a tremor.

A trail of metronome,
& the abalone smell of her, contagious, silver.

A knot
of rope, heavy, the color of oysters, affixed

at the throat.
His timely thumbs drenched in paraffin wax.

Fog on the film. I said, my bones are gone.
He poured me, like fluid, into glass.

LAS CRUCES

It's no longer the heft of persimmons
that wreaks her heart. A small

and giddy thing
seems only small and giddy.

In the thicket of sleep
(you wanted the baby, don't you?)

all English is broken.
Border towns of citrus and blood.
He watches

her cleanse her palette.

HERITAGE

It means I found a home where I was dropped.
The churlish heron
looming on the bridge, keeping stock—
Abandoned summer boats
in dry docks. Nestled, hull

to hull. Like the sand-soft husks of a walnut.
When you die, I don't think that I will go. Not even then.

He understands, & the night infused with violets.

MEXICAN FIRE OPAL

The most
indelicate idea
the sun could make.

How come gladioli

are always obscuring
the story? As a child
would flush—

PRONE, NOVEMBER

Just your slow, pink movements near the doorway.

If there were fields, they'd long ago rolled back in agate bliss.
Until you were indelible, a dahlia.

Bale of hay, almost made for a woman bent over.
Her pale, sweet hedging (which,

in certain landscapes,
is an early form of love).

I want you slow: birds hover near my waist.

Not sleep in the distance but the mimeograph
of sleep.

Above all else, the trembling resembles a forest.

BIRTH BELL

The beginning of war was also a blossom. Here's
where you started to finger

your terrible pearls. Undoing the want

takes a long, long time. Sometimes
you never. Days spent

circumventing bougainvillea.
Flash forward

to those Indiana fields, those stray dogs,
the idling truck.

You could stroke their fur forever and nothing would change.

ATTIC SERIES

Where were you when the wind was in shackles?
Face down on the mattress,
munching on dust. Three out of four

rooms in the house were ablaze or aghast.
Hear the murmuring birds?

I can feel their bones shifting, you said.

Hush, now. Pick up the pace.
(It's a movement of war.) Try to steer him
with your thighs,
make the document manic.

BLANC DE CHINE, AKA THE WONDERMENT

You like your houses with nobody in them. Where creosote

groans in the alley. Where dust is not dust.
Is ochre, nacre, bone.

Maybe you'll wear
what you've done
on the outside now, like so much

perilous jewelry. Your face
is like a house that no one owns.

EVEN STARLINGS

I've been thinking a lot about will. How it serves
and doesn't serve us. The heart stammers on with her luggage,
silk lining a witness. Takes her things and just goes home.

Like watching geese continue to struggle, long after the crumb was gone.
Those geese were wrong. But their feathers are soft and white
as the sheath of death.

Somewhere, the world's smallest boy is rowing a boat.
His boat is too small, and he rows too hard.
I try to imagine

even starlings have a purpose.
It's a good year for stealing babies, so I hear.

CLAVICLE

Lonely, wasn't it.
Here comes your father, wearing his exit trousers.
I knew a lot about bones, back then. Trying to not
imagine the end of sleep.
Folding my gloves so the fingers were basically gone.

Imagine somebody speaks, but they've not got hands.
Flute and *ravine* and *permission*.

Imagine this box of feathers
contains the only love that's left.

THE CARTESIAN OTHER

In the narrowest spaces, she doth unravel, as if
a forest fire.

In its simplest form, *starving*: lack of food

but also (archaic) to bludgeon with cold.

& the lake
like a Molotov cocktail…

The dominant color always flame.

MARIPOSA DE LA MUERTE

Pupae were placed
in the mouths of the victims.

With my back against the wall
I can see this for what it was—

the pursuit of velvet.

TWO

REMNANT

There was the gale-white surgeon's lamp,
a man in scrubs.

The dark, derivative afterbirth
of joy, first kin

of deception. Some women cried, handing each other snow.
They couldn't get their babies back or didn't want to.

There is no place for us
to walk towards the light. Nor,

the harbored influence of trees.

But I was laid out on the table, see.
With a care that was foreign.

IMPRINT

Everyone has one: the dominion of down.
Your giving in

is a kind of willed amnesia,
the color of a rabbit's underfur.

To speak of a word like *bait.* You were young,

among the horses.
To make of your mouth an "O,"
the landscape getting

all flustered. There's the theory
of the girl, the one that

was holding wisteria.

Which, when you get right
down to it, strangles trees.

SATINE

I know there were years

I lived in the valley

of what couldn't be true.

But how to explain

the way its inhabitants called me? His violent way

of looking at the world,

the way the hummingbird's chin

was indigo in light, then suddenly, marauders.

How I fingered my ruffles and wept. You could say it was wrong,

but the moment seemed grosgrain and urgent. So I hung

my belief on a hook (little noose).

Like a slip you might leave at his place;

what was once

so pale and alive there.

LOCKET

At first, I wouldn't believe:
calla lilies dipped in pink, but only the tips,
like a small girl's toes, like the bell curve of crave.
How the clinking of teeth

tastes slightly of antique silver, of April in Denver.
Collared doves I watched in their cage.
How their color is buff, a low-lying fog,
the uncertain shore of childhood. But the black

at their necks is so fixed.
Is the adult kohl at my eyes,
is your hair, mink sky around us,
wild & fixed.

THE MORAINES

I think of the year I spent not watching birds:

sky crosshatched with trauma, skin-graft-pink,
the L.A. sun, an ebullient and misinformed satsuma

finally being engulfed by the smog-filled sky—
So why would anyone shake

their head in wonder? Like giving an affidavit
to the blind.

BUREAU OF RECLAMATION

(Salton City, California)

Our dream of wayward gulls,
exhausted stars

calibrating, indiscriminately—

Waves skirting
the skiffs.

Cormorants
drying their wings. Zinnias or witches?

(How witches persist.)

The animal smell of *pollute*: make a list

of atmospheres
you're willing

to believe in. I like my eggs with DDT. I like you behind me,
on pale, marine-layer mornings.

STILL

Good to live
where the stars still work. A little
cirrus/nimbus floating by—

Confess: you wanted the world (and you)

to just shut up.
And what is there to say? *He posed*
me like a dead girl and I liked it.

OCCAM'S RAZOR

They say it is because

you're lost in grief. As though it were a place you could move out of

if you only had the map.

The un-locatable nowhere
notwithstanding.

Where the road cuts through the quarry, halcyon ruse.

TRUE NORTH

There is a small land we call Heaven.
The does are indeterminable but warm.
Perhaps the smallest

thinks she can see Canada. A
last lonely light

on in Halifax. *Estuarine:*

it's the progress of blood at your wrist.
Or the way I can open you up

then watch you close.
It's the grass that worries, what

if we don't need her anymore.
In the meantime, only endless chambers.

The hipbone under your skin
that someone dealt.

ELK RIVER ROAD

(Humboldt County, California)

Like the last of the damned, a handful,
slender bay—

It's true I had wondered: marigolds growing
all over

this locked door.
Excited (admit it)

by the voile of the drapes.
Fluttering

all, *farmer-ly*.

The role of the marigolds, the voile.

MEMENTO MORI

Sometimes she'd look at me, anew. I wanted to say,
You're dying, don't you know? Stroke

a silky ribbon 'til it curls. It is tender

on occasion, to be firm. I thought of a tabby,
dragging her kittens by the scruff.

The twinkling St. Christopher
placed in the palm of my hand. Or I thought

of the verb "to long" for far too long. Dark plaintiff,
rapping his fingers at your door.

If my father loved her, all the evidence is gone.
Subsequent wife

shreds photos, her own heart. *Patron Saint
of Hailstorms, Travelers, Spurn.*

THE CANARY

Few coins in a paper cup. Rattle them slowly.
So this

is living alone; the pale heart
shards. Long nights, I watched my mother tweeze
her legs, not wincing once. Divorce

can make you lucky,
like the odds.

If you ask me to loosen my grip,
consider the source—
My father put his right hand through the glass.

It was yellow & soft,
my mother's lamplit hair.

I couldn't keep my hands off the canary.

SEA CRIMES

Now listen to me good. To be dreaming
of the cove, the light pink cottage
that was always on the edge. This being the year

my jeans fell from my frame. You said I was closer to God
but he wouldn't concur. Weeds

grew up on bales of clean, white salt. All summer
everyone wondered

where I lived, watched the carpenter ants on the rocks.
When I wasn't in my body, I was dead. Cops

circled, paraphernalia swirled
inside my lonely purse.

There was nothing to do but wait.
Contraband, will you
turn to silk again? Tilt his white, Atlantic
throat up

to the shy-eyed puffins?

ORION

I hear you left your virtue by the harbor.
But the children keep appearing,

large and white. Inexplicable,
like cargo isn't mine.

Ever stumble
onto a nest of roaches? It was like that,

when you left. At first

the motion startles,
then the mass.

TWENTYNINE PALMS

For the days when beauty was elsewhere.
Someone beats off

in the trailer, it's the stellar white dream:
cocaine and long-stemmed brides.

Always, you must focus on the sky. Bougainvillea
mutely moving like a stain, a young girl

peeing in the pool.

Is that what you wanted? Subtle? The lukewarm
politics of someone else's marriage?

FORM

Maybe you forget these pointless hills.

And the horse that gulped down air in the one good year

of the excellence of its greed.

When his fingers were on me, I felt a violence

open called loving him back.

Which is to say, it's a difficult place here, God.

Do you relate more to the dove or the snake?

Would you rather be harmless or stupid?

FATE IS THE HUNTER

Blind shoots and restrainer systems. The procession
is curved, scientifically

proven to help keep your eyes on the rump
of the one in the front. Lest
you have knowledge.

Here's what I think about knowledge—
At night I take off my blush,
which is pink as meat.

MIMEOGRAPH

Marked snow folds over the threshold.
I hedge my bets, one white pill on the tongue.
& when we

talk, it's a kind of silent
choreography.
As animals will cluster
for their warmth.

Their metallic breath
holds a version of the secret. Each print grows,

less and less.

CONFISCATE

Remember the night we filled the motel
room with razors. You threw
my high heel

in a field, & watched me sweat. Who said

we wanted: division of sky
& land, delineation—

I don't know how the fields can be so casual.
By then, you were swinging

over a swimming hole. A raven following,
closely behind you.

Precarious raven. Precarious bird.

RINGLET

While you were busy
qualifying butterflies. Taking the liminal stretch

of each pinked wing. Fawn is a soundtrack for beauty. Wood nymphs,
meadow browns, ringlets. Jezebels, parchment, pins.

Outside: the sound of the sun
becoming more of what she was—

the velvet slug of their bodies (Nabokov

said they were girls).

But also, I wanted to tell you
there are winds that you won't own.

There's a file on you, somewhere—

Stiff corridor, this.

SNOWDROP

The first abandonment was birth. But just admit it,
there were snowdrops all along.

White nurses, linoleum floor. Abstract
gleam of disinfectant.

They couldn't show you, in those days,
for your own good. They were twisting

the arm of God. They
were wrapping it up, in a blanket like a lamb.

You, who kept your shoes on, navy blue. How they bobbed,
like small, warned boats,

each time he was in you.

HEART OF GLASS

You were damp whorls, you were terror.
Lilac pines for orris,

for the company of men.

I see that I only get what the snow un-lies.

May the columbine
grow in the salt hills, may it poison your children.

Through all of this, I'll remain. Ever so.
Sylvan.

Though the forest will grow sparse
as a beggar's dress.

FOUR DRIVES IN THE HEART OF THE DESERT

Went out to the edge of my life. Tumbled soft,
by wind and by sun, by ocean, by elsewhere, Anza

Borrego—
Less of a schism

between man and sky, less democracy really.

Remembered the terrible theatre

of the rental car, that summer, my father
turning slowly into lava. This is the country

they say, where no one can live. Shed it

like shale. Where stars will refuse

to fasten themselves to the sky,
will stream down in contrails

& stammer.

SILT

Yes, it was a kind of terror. As if fingering
the spine of a book, then finding
every page is gone.   In this admission,
children *can* go missing,

houses burn. No one comes.

The other version is this: the road goes on forever,
lined in ocotillo, pure hot tarmac
throughout the valley,
along the skeleton coast—

ACKNOWLEDGMENTS

Thanks to the editors and staff of the following publications where some of these poems originally appeared, sometimes in slightly different forms.

Anti—, Aesthetix, Barn Owl Review, Barrow Street, Blackbird, DIAGRAM, Diode, Inlandia, The Laurel Review, Many Mountains Moving, Massachusetts Review, Ninth Letter, Octopus, Perihelion, Route Seven Review, Third Coast, The Offending Adam, Triquarterly, Zocolo Public Square.

Some of these poems also appeared in the chapbook *Above All Else, the Trembling Resembles a Fores*t, Burnside Review Press, 2010.

"The 10:15 to Cambridge" is in memory of Ann Manson.

During the time I was writing this book I was cheered on by many friends. I hope you know who you are; you helped make it possible.

My deepest thanks to everyone at Four Way Books, especially Ryan Murphy and Martha Rhodes.

DDL—In art and in life: thank you and love.

NOTES

"Fate is the Hunter" makes reference to Temple Grandin's theory of slaughterhouse design.

"Heart of Glass" is composed entirely of subtitles from the film of the same name, directed by Werner Herzog.

Louise Mathias was born in Bedford, England, and grew up in England and Los Angeles. She is the author of *Lark Apprentice*, chosen by Brenda Hillman for the New Issues Poetry Prize and published by New Issues Press in 2004, as well as a chapbook, *Above All Else, the Trembling Resembles a Forest*, which won the Burnside Review Chapbook contest. Her poems have appeared in *Barrow Street*, *Massachusetts Review*, *Octopus*, *TriQuarterly*, and many other journals. She splits her time between Joshua Tree, California, a small town in the Mojave Desert, and Northern Indiana.